THEY AND WE WILL GET INTO TROUBLE FOR THIS

THEY AND
WE WILL
GET INTO
TROUBLE
FOR THIS

ANNA MOSCHOVAKIS

COFFEE HOUSE PRESS

MINNEAPOLIS

2016

Coffee House Press books are available to the trade through our primary distributor, Consortium. For book sales and distribution, contact cbsd.com or (800) 283-3572. For personal orders, catalogs, or other information, write to info@coffeehousepress.org.

Coffee House Press is a nonprofit literary publishing house. Support from private foundations, corporate giving programs, government programs, and generous individuals helps make the publication of our books possible. We gratefully acknowledge their support in detail in the back of this book.

PERMISSIONS

The 'needs inventory' on page 46 is borrowed from the Center for Nonviolent Communication, © 2005.

'Flat White (20/20)' is based on a translation of 'Café sans sucre' by Samira Negrouche, originally published in *Le jazz des oliviers* (Editions du Tell, Blida), © 2010. Adapted with permission from Samira Negrouche.

Excerpts from 'On Being Numerous' by George Oppen are from *New Collected Poems*, © 1968 by George Oppen. Adapted with permission from New Directions Publishing Corp.

LIBRARY OF CONGRESS CATALOGING-IN-PUBLICATION DATA

Moschovakis, Anna, author.
[Poems. Selections]
They and we will get into trouble for this : poems / Anna Moschovakis.
pages cm
ISBN 978-1-56689-420-3 (paperback)
I. Title.
PS3613.O7787A6 2015
811'.6—dc23
2015028946

PRINTED IN THE UNITED STATES OF AMERICA

23 22 21 20 19 18 17 16   1 2 3 4 5 6 7 8

For my grandmothers, Gertrude and Ismene

[WHAT IS HAPPENING IN THE ROOM] [HOW WE ARE IN THE ROOM]

[WHAT IS HAPPENING IN THE ROOM] [HOW WE ARE IN THE ROOM

] [THE ROOM IS FULL] [THE ROOM IS UNBREAKING] [THE ROOM IS

BROKE] [HOW IS THE ROOM] [WE ARE] [IN THE ROOM] [WHAT

PARADISE
(FILM TWO)

IS HAPPENING] [IN THE ROOM] [BRACKETED] [BY CONVICTION]

/\/\/\/\/ [THE ROOM IS VIBRATING] [OF PEOPLE W/ BROWN HAIR]

I don't know a thing about paradise || In my house nobody ever brought it up || In college I learned about Kierkegaard's knights || the knight of resignation || and the knight of faith || I wanted to be a knight of faith || as did the professor || and everyone else in the class || I assumed || I was born in paradise || and raised in science || The semester I studied Kierkegaard || I also took calculus || which I failed || I fell in love || with the sounds of cypresses || in the wind || There is the female cypress || and the male cypress || and it was the male I loved || That same semester I also read || *The Symposium* || by Plato || in Walter Hamilton's English translation || You will remember

[OF PEOPLE W/ PALE] [SKIN] [OF PEOPLE W/ PALE HAIR] [BROWN

The Symposium || is about a dinner party || and you are familiar || with the story in it || told by the comedian || Aristophanes || about the search for love || the origin of longing || how we have all been split in two || broken || each half doomed to wander || 'far and wide' || in search of || the other || We refer to this story || which Socrates belittled || in common expressions || like 'She completes me' || and || 'How is your better half?' || and even when we refer || to finding 'the one' || or our 'soul mate' || In the culture in which I was raised || after premarital sex || divorce and remarriage || became accepted || then commonplace || it became possible to find || your soul mate || not just once || but twice

SKIN] [THE ROOM IS VIBRATING OF] [PEOPLE W/ SKIN] [HAIR]

three times or more || and to declare it to the world || across platforms || even || in a church || Anxiety over this development || which may be described || using a term I learned || the same semester || I flunked calculus || read Kierkegaard || Theresa Hak Kyung Cha || and *The Symposium* || as a 'paradigm shift' || is pervasive || if unacknowledged || for how can you find || your other half || more than once || They say || the human body || regenerates itself || every seven years || By 'they' I mean 'modern' || 'science' || and in the fifth century before Christ || Heraclitus wrote || δὶς ἐς τὸν αὐτὸν ποταμὸν οὐκ ἂν ἐμβαίης || which we are told means || you can't step in the same river

[TO BE RADICALLY] [REFT] [OPEN BRACKET] [TO BE] [REFT]

twice || The conventional marriage ceremony || derived from the Catholics || still calls for the promise || to remain || for richer or poorer || for better or for worse || in sickness and in health || etcetera || Being raised in science || under the sign of logic || I never understood how certain promises || could be made || I could say 'I promise || that unless something unexpected happens || I will do the dishes every night || this week' || I was very literal || especially with my lovers || I could say 'I love you today' || but not 'I will love you tomorrow' || 'I'm in this || for the long haul' || I would have made a terrible || bride || which might be why || the only marriage proposal || I received was on a transatlantic phone call || with an unhinged person || who knew I would say no || I had a good relationship || with a philosopher || fall irrevocably apart || over my inability to perform || what I had learned to call || 'speech acts' || a term coined by J. L. Austin || and developed || by John Searle || whose class I also took || in college || though sometime after || the disaster of || the calculus || I went to paradise with a friend || Hope || During our stay another friend || went home to Ohio || with his camera || sent a photo || HELL IS REAL || across a billboard || which I received || on my phone || Growing up I watched a show || on public television || 'Connections' in which the host followed a trail || wherever it led || across time || space || and disciplinary divides || This before the invention || of hypertext markup language || broadband || FOMO || or the smartphone || 'Connections' || was a big 'influence' || on my 'work' || Freud said the two things || most important in life || are love and work || I'm paraphrasing || having never read Freud || at least not the part where he wrote || about this || I am working in paradise || There's a bird here that makes || a noise like a typewriter || Smith Corona or Olivetti || a manual || I don't know what bird it is || I don't know the story || of Adam and Eve || except in its vulgar outline || I have thought about reading it || in the bible || but there are so many other books || I want to get to || first || I thought || I could kill two || birds with one stone || so to speak || by reading it in || French || to practice my comprehension || so that in some sense it would constitute || work || I turn pages under birds || of paradise || try to find the passage || can't || There is one story from the bible || I know quite well || the one about Abraham || and his son Isaac || I know it from its appearance || in *Fear and Trembling* || by Kierkegaard || I did find the story || of Abraham and Isaac || in the bible || It's in Genesis || I was surprised || at how short it was || and by some of the || wording || 'Or, après ces événements || Dieu mit Abraham à l'épreuve || et lui dit: "Abraham"; il repondit; "Me voici." || Il reprit: "Prends ton fils, ton unique, Isaac, que tu aimes. || Pars pour le pays de Moriyya || et là, tu l'offriras en holocauste || sur celle des montagnes || que je t'indiquerai.'" || I was surprised by the use of the word || 'holocauste' || when the word I expected was || 'sacrifice' || a word that does exist in French || spelled just as in English || with the identical dictionary || definition || I made a note to go || to the library || back home || or the Internet I guess || to look at King James || and see what word is there || It occured to me also || that I'd never wondered || at the origin of the word

] [THERE IS CHANGE / IN AN AIR / THAT SMELLS STALE, THEY WILL

'holocaust' || before it came to refer || to the genocides of World War II || thousands of years after Abraham || was talked into murder || and a century after Kierkegaard || wrote || under a pseudonym || Johannes de silentio || his *Fear and Trembling* || The story of Abraham and Isaac is || five paragraphs long || is told simply || without psychologizing || The characters are affectless || It's like a script || waiting for actors || to fill it with || emotion || When Freud said love and work || I assume he meant meaningful || work || but it still seems || further definition || is required || When I say I'm working || in paradise || I refer to one kind || of work || to the writing of this || film which you are now || watching || finding meaningful || I hope || as I found meaning in the process || of its creation || Another type of work || I perform in paradise || is cleaning || mostly dishwashing || which I enjoy but || do not find particularly || meaningful || and yet another type of work || I perform || is the intensive pruning || of olive trees || in an ancient || olive grove || which I both enjoy || and find meaningful || since it allows me || to commune || with nature || and with a notion || of the past || I am not paid for this work || I was not paid to go to paradise || In fact I covered || my room and board || and volunteered my || labor || There are ten episodes of || 'Connections' || ten lines per page of this poem || ten commandments || tribes || And he || Boaz || took ten men || of the elders || as judges and said || Sit down || and they sat || Medea || sacrificed || both of her children || though no god asked her to || and unlike Abraham she has rarely || been praised for the intention || much less the execution || of this act || In a film version of *Medea* || by Lars von Trier || the scene of the execution || is filled with emotion || though stark || wordless || 'It is written on their faces' || EXT. HILL—DAY: Woman ascends hill || her sons in her arms || While Abraham believed Isaac || after the sacrifice || would rise to paradise || or so I assume || Medea would not have been afforded

[WAY—THERE IS SOMETHING] [IN THE CORNER] [A BLANK] [FOR

such comfort || the Greeks holding || a different conception || of paradise || a place inhabited by gods || inaccessible to mortals || even after death || This || along with the fact that Medea's || reasons for killing her children || were essentially || or at least ostensibly || selfish || make her act appear less || like a sacrifice and more || like slaughter || After God spares Abraham the agony || of killing his only son || 'qu'il aime' || a ram appears || and Abraham kills it || instead || 'Il alla le prendre pour l'offrir || en holocauste || à la place de son fils.' || We are told that Abraham named this place || 'le seigneur voit' || and reminded it's still common to say 'c'est sur || la montagne

TRAINING SHOOTERS TO SEE] [OTHER SHOOTERS] [ENTANGLED]

que le seigneur est vu' || a phrase rendered || in the King James version of the bible as || 'in the mount of the Lord || it shall be seen' || but in other, more recent || versions as || 'on the mountain of the Lord || it will be provided' || a translation that brings out the 'hold' || in 'behold' || the link between seeing || and having for keeps || I don't know how the passage || reads in || *The Message: The Bible* || *in Contemporary Language* || published in 2005 || and rated on average || 4.5 stars || in more than 900 customer || reviews || but I know that each year || on the anniversary of his death || Martin Luther King Jr. proclaims || on the airwaves || he's been to the mountain || is not fearing any || man || That Medea

[THEY] [THE ABSOLUTE SINGULAR] [THEY] [OF THE SINGULAR]

killed her children || whom she loved || deliberately || was a revision of the traditional myth || which itself had alternate endings || one claiming their deaths were an accident || the other || blaming the citizens || of Corinth || neither of which appears || to have been sufficiently tragic || for the playwright Euripedes || who added in || fillicide || 'Holocaust' it turns out || does mean 'sacrifice || to the gods' || or || etymologically || something like 'burnt whole' || The preferred term for the extermination of Jews is now 'Shoah' || for 'catastrophe' || the Greek origin of which || combines 'down' with || 'turn' || as in 'a sudden end' || or 'reversal of the || expected' || a definition || that emphasizes || the result of the thing || the plot over the act || the work || of slaughter || I don't know if it's accurate || or appropriate to draw || a correlation || between the mountain in MLK's speech || and the mountain || in Genesis 22 || The professor who taught me Kierkegaard || Dreyfus || seemed to make the connection || between King and Abraham || by suggesting || as I recall || that both would qualify || under Kierkegaard's definition || as knights of faith || able to see || the dagger hanging || over their beloveds || and not recoil || but love || the more fiercely || There's a danger || of sentimentality || in this view || to be weighed against the danger || of the critique of || sentiment || There's a library || in paradise || and in it a book || *Disbelief and Faith Are Not What You Think* || written by someone || named Jean-François Six || I liked his name || and the fact that in French the title || *L'Incroyance et la foi ne sont pas ce qu'on croit* || rhymes || 'This book,' he writes || 'is an invitation to || an experimental faith || a humble, vulnerable faith' || In another book I found || the etymology of the term || 'entrainment' || used in certain psychoanalytic texts || to describe the transmission of affect between || individuals || in other words, contagion || suggesting we are not contained || within the contours of our || bodies || the outlines || of our skin || The language of halfness in Aristophanes' speech || may be an attempt to explain

CALLY] [REFT] [MOTION] [TO HAVE STIMULATED THE NEURONAL

metaphorically || hence inaccurately || and well before Freud and the dawn of psychoanalysis || this fluidity of boundaries || 'Entraîner' || the infinitive of the French 'entraînement' || means simply 'to train' || as in || for the Olympics || or || for success || in love || It turns out the last || line in the marriage liturgy || originates from the Book of Common Prayer || 1549 || where it read || 'till death us departe' || so different to my ear || from its 1662 || replacement || 'till death us do part' || as the former seems to emphasize || the 'us' of the departure || the tearing asunder || of both || from earth || and not || of one from || the other || and I retain that sense of distinction || even after learning || that the meaning of the phrases || is the same || It turns out my understanding || such as it is || of tragedy || was shaped || during that fateful semester || less by the Greeks than by Cha || the only woman writer I remember || being assigned || It turns out Heraclitus || never said the thing || about stepping into the river again || that it was probably a disciple || forgotten by history || or some poor scribe || bursting with inspiration || I was alerted to this fallacy || as well as to the fact || that 'kierkegaard' || means 'churchyard' || in the philosopher's native Danish || years later || by the novelist David Markson || another 'influence' || on my 'work' || a knight of resignation || perhaps || who is now || here with us in

THE ROOM] [AND WHAT IS HAPPENING] [THE NEURONAL SYNAPS-

paradise || Entraîner: to pull or to carry || away or along; || to train; || to lead (to); || to cause; bring about || an invitation || to a faith || a humble || experiment || an influence || the necessity || of its critique || When I went to paradise || it rained || for ten days straight || I walked up the hill || to the mountaintop || The olive grove || flooded || for forty nights || I forgot the word || for a poem with ten lines || but you can look it up || from most anywhere || If you want to know || I failed to follow || instructions || I got lost for a while || This was years ago || I forgot || my camera || and had to take || pictures || on my phone || I shared them with everyone || and saved them all || for myself

ES CAUSE LACK] [OF CONVICTION] [OR INCREASED] [CONVICTION

] [ALONG WITH A SENSE OF] [AND ALSO] [EMOTION] [TO HAVE

WHAT IT MEANS
TO BE
AVANT-GARDE

(after David Antin)

STIMULATED] [WETHEY IN A ROOM] [WETHEY ARE HAPPENING IN

] [THE ROOM] [RADICALLY] [REFT] [OF THE ABSOLUTE] /\/\/\/\/

I feel sad.

I feel discouraged about the future.

I feel I have failed more than the average person.

As I look back on my life, all I can see is a lot of failures.

I don't get real satisfaction out of anything anymore.

I am dissatisfied or bored with everything.

I feel quite guilty most of the time.

I expect to be punished.

I am disgusted with myself.

I am critical of myself for my weaknesses or mistakes.

I blame myself for everything bad that happens.

I have thoughts of killing myself, but I would not carry them out.

I would like to kill myself.

I would kill myself if I had the chance.

I don't cry any more than usual.

I used to be able to cry, but now I can't cry even though I want to.

I am no more irritated by things than I ever was.

I am slightly more irritated now than usual.

I have lost all of my interest in other people.

I make decisions about as well as I ever could.

I can't make decisions at all anymore.

I am worried that I am looking old or unattractive.

I feel there are permanent changes in my appearance that make me look

    unattractive.

[WHAT IS HAPPENING] [WHAT IS THE DIFFERENCE] [BETWEEN THE

I have to push myself very hard to do anything.

I don't sleep as well as I used to.

I wake up several hours earlier than I used to and cannot get back to sleep.

I get tired from doing almost anything.

My appetite is not as good as it used to be.

My appetite is much worse now.

I have lost more than five pounds.

I have lost more than fifteen pounds.

I am worried about physical problems like aches, pains, upset stomach, or constipation.

I am very worried about physical problems and it's hard to think of much else.

I have not noticed any recent change in my interest in sex.

I have lost interest in sex completely.

DIFFERENCE] [BETWEEN ONE PERSON AND ANOTHER] [THINKING

I was in the park when they called —— with my head on my knee and my nose in a book —— the book was by David Antin, an American —— there are many ways to follow a thought —— when the phone rang they told me they wanted me —— there was a voice on the phone that belonged to a man —— it sounded like a man and him saying they wanted me —— I read a book the other day by a circus performer —— in my youth I read a book by an anthropologist's son —— who ran off with the Gypsies with his parents' blessing —— the anthropologist's son was not an American —— the circus performer was unstable emotionally —— she committed suicide at the age of forty-two —— the man said we want you to come in for some tests —— the parents hoped the boy would grow up to write a book —— in which he'd detail the functioning of Romani culture —— before the phone rang I was reading the bit in the Antin —— about how it's a good thing to be on the fringe —— the boy learned the Gypsies don't lie to their own —— coterie makes you soft —— when I went in for the tests they said I was normal —— and only after I did a lot of research on the Internet —— did I come to understand what they meant by that —— was that my condition is unexplained

] [DIFFERENCE] [AND THE DIFFERENCE BETWEEN ONE PERSON AND

I feel downhearted and blue Most of the time.

Morning is when I feel the best Some of the time.

I have crying spells or feel like it Good part of the time.

I have trouble sleeping at night A little of the time.

I eat as much as I used to Good part of the time.

I still enjoy sex A little of the time.

I notice that I am losing weight Some of the time.

I have trouble with constipation A little of the time

My heart beats faster than usual Some of the time.

I get tired for no reason Good part of the time.

My mind is as clear as it used to be A little of the time.

I find it easy to do the things I used to Some of the time.

I am restless and can't keep still Most of the time.

I feel hopeful about the future A little of the time.

I am more irritable than usual Most of the time.

I find it easy to make decisions [   ]

I feel that I am useful and needed Some of the time.

My life is pretty full A little of the time.

I feel that others would be better off if I were dead Most of the time.

I still enjoy the things I used to do [   ]

ONE] [MACHINE] [HE WONDERED ALOUD] [SUICIDALLY] [THE

I had forgotten the name of the anthropologist's son —— it was mid-
morning and I was sitting at my desk —— taking the last sip
of my morning decaf with soy —— the last sip is always cold
and unsatisfying —— this was not my first attempt to recover
the boy's name —— I had of course forgotten the book's title as
well —— I typed Dutch Gypsy narrative young anthropologist
into my machine —— for fifteen years I've been trying to
recall the name of the boy or of the book —— I may even have
unsuccessfully searched for them before —— during those years
I recreated a memory of the narrative —— he is beloved by the
group and accepted as one of them —— he does not miss his
parents though he holds them in high esteem —— he learns to
sing from a dark-haired man and to steal from a dark-haired
girl —— the boy himself is as blond as a broom —— the feeling
of not knowing is like flying in your dreams —— around the
time I started searching I stopped dreaming anything fun ——
Dutch Gypsy narrative young anthropologist did the trick
—— his name came up and I remembered it —— recognition
makes you fall but you can try to resist —— though you'll make
yourself ridiculous flapping all around —— I switched windows
and searched for my unexplained condition —— there are lots
of people who have it and none of them can spell —— it turns
out I was wrong about my search being successful —— the

ROOM BRACKETED] [COLD] [WHAT IS HAPPENING HERE THE] [

name I thought I recognized was of a different person —— an
eighteenth-century abolitionist who fell in love with a slave ——
he slept with many others but only fell in love once —— I did
another search and this time left out nationality —— I typed son
of anthropologists adopted by Gypsies —— when mysteries
are explained they don't exactly disappear —— the boy was
Belgian not Dutch and that had been my mistake —— the man
called back to say one of my test results was compromised ——
the title of the book is *The Gypsies*

Feeling nervous, anxious, or on edge Nearly every day.

Not being able to stop or control worrying More than half the days.

Worrying too much about different things Several days.

Trouble relaxing More than half the days.

Being so restless that it's hard to sit still Several days.

Becoming easily annoyed or irritable Nearly every day.

Feeling afraid, as if something awful might

The Gypsies was republished in 1987 —— a time that still can be called

my youth —— I was living in Los Angeles waiting for high school

to end —— my condition would not manifest for another twenty

years —— in the talk where David Antin discusses life on the

fringe —— he is in Los Angeles at an art space called LACE ——

I don't know what year it was but I could have been there ——

growing up in a metropolis can make you soft —— I've been

going to the same art institutions most of my life —— you have

the sense you should be heading inevitably for the center ——

when people ask me where I live I say the middle of nowhere

—— under certain circumstances it requires effort to stay on

the fringe —— what we're told about Gypsies is they make no

home —— in 1957 David Antin was living in Manhattan —— in

an apartment that cost him $18.50 a month —— when I moved

to Manhattan it was 1993 —— the same year Antin's talk on the

fringe would be published —— I paid $400 a month to live in

the East Village —— I fell in love with a cook at the restau-

rant where I waitressed —— he carried a knife on the subway

because his city was dangerous —— he made me feel totally

irrevocably Californian —— the blizzard that winter was record

breaking —— we spent our nights at the restaurant and our

days in the darkroom —— we woke in strangers' apartments on

Avenue D —— we buried two friends in a matter of months ——

IN] [LET IN DEATH] [DON'T LET DEATH IN] [LET IN DEATH] [OF

sometimes an image moves to the center of a life —— his mother and stepfather were trained anthropologists —— looking now at the pictures I can see we were happy —— when we broke up he asked if I was leaving him for art —— eventually he became an editor at *Rolling Stone* —— we had a drink at a bar and I explained my condition —— he gave me many books during our four years together —— one of them was *The Gypsies*

ONE SORT BUT NOT] [OF ANOTHER] [SORT] [FOR THE SAKE OF

I can easily tell if someone else wants to enter a conversation Strongly agree

I prefer animals to humans Strongly disagree

I try to keep up with the current trends and fashions Mildly agree

I dream most nights No answer

I really enjoy caring for other people.

I try to solve my own problems rather than discussing them with others.

I find it hard to know what to do in a social situation.

I am at my best first thing in the morning.

It doesn't bother me too much if I am late meeting a friend.

I would never break a law, no matter how minor.

I often find it difficult to judge if something is rude or polite.

I prefer practical jokes to verbal humor.

If I see a stranger in a group, I think it's up to them to make an effort to join in.

I usually stay emotionally detached when watching a film.

I can easily work out what another person might want to talk about.

I can tell if someone is masking their true emotion.

Before making a decision I always weigh the pros and cons.

I live for today rather than for the future.

THE ROOM FOR] [WHAT] [IS BEING MADE TO HAPPEN] [HERE]

In 'the fringe' David Antin talks about the white light —— if you were raised in the center you know what he means —— if you were born on the fringe I can't know what you know —— despite my high score on the empathy quotient test —— devised by a doctor named Simon Baron-Cohen —— a psychologist from Cambridge with two brothers in show biz —— directors of independent British films —— another white light —— bright but not blinding —— like the one that shines on their cousin Sacha —— sued for libel by the Roma in 2006 —— still the white light shines from name to name —— empathy has been theorized in many ways —— the first I encountered was that of David Hume —— though he doesn't use the word, instead splitting 'sympathy' —— into a complex mode of experience —— in which the process of understanding is reversed —— from impression → idea —— to idea → impression —— there are many ways to think about loss —— the Roma are known to originate in India —— not Egypt or Romania as once was believed —— thus the misnomer 'Gypsy,' and its derivative slurs —— and still there are 'Gypsies' living in India —— I've read they make their livings selling broomsticks and tools —— except the ones committed to religious begging —— many people from the white light of LA or New York —— take journeys to India to study yoga for example —— I know some of them and they are very nice people

[BE REFT] [OF ONE SORT BUT NOT] [ANOTHER] [SORT] [LET

—— I imagine they score high on the empathy quotient test ——
what I'm trying to get at is impossible to say —— the people we
bury put us in the ground too —— from impression to idea and
back again —— the grounding is temporary and we eventually
'move on' —— I heard some bad news when I woke up this
morning —— my condition had faded to the back of my mind
—— the news came from a friend, a translator from India —— a
new friend I'd met on the organized fringe —— I never knew
life would be so much about death —— I wrote to him that there
were no words for his suffering —— a tautological statement
with a paradox at its heart —— a week ago we all sat together on
the grass —— indulging in the first warm rays of spring sun ——
the translator was the only one sitting in the shade —— this he
attributed to the heat in his country of origin —— Calcutta may
as well be the middle of nowhere —— it never has topped my list
of places to visit —— now empathy has made me want to get on
a plane —— I wonder if this is what Antin means —— to be alive
in the perfectly reasonable shabby human light —— my hand
ahead of my heart ahead of my hand

IN DEATH] [THERE BE] [TROUBLE] [THERE IS] [HAPPENING IN

crossed arms (folded arms)   Defensiveness, reluctance

crossed arms with clenched fists   Hostile defensiveness

gripping own upper arms   Insecurity

one arm across body clasping other arm by side (female)   Nervousness

arms held behind body with hands clasped   Confidence, authority

handbag held in front of body (female)   Nervousness

holding papers across chest (mainly male)   Nervousness

adjusting cuff, watchstrap, tie, etc., using an arm across the body   Nervousness

arms/hands covering genital region (male)   Nervousness

holding a drink in front of body with both hands   Nervousness

seated, holding drink on one side with hand from other side   Nervousness

touching or scratching shoulder using arm across body   Nervousness

THE WARM MACHINE] [OF THE ROOM] [ABSOLUTE] [TROUBLE]

Just as I was getting to the part about Vietnam —— I misplaced Antin's book in a series of moves —— there was a time when I might just have ordered another —— but that was before the economic crash of the aughts —— so I am left to imagine what connections should be drawn —— between the war, the fringe, and the blinding white light —— what we know about connections is they're often wrong —— in high school I lived in Athens, Greece —— a capital city if there ever was one —— some Gypsies made their home a few blocks from our apartment —— an unofficial country on waterfront land —— that was before the economic boom of the nineties —— and the amenities necessitated by the coming Olympics —— during one of my moves I found a copy of *The Tourist* —— the newer edition with a foreword by Lucy Lippard —— the question of staged authenticity had been on my mind —— in her foreword Lippard admits to having a bad memory —— which she relies on to allow her to do some thinking of her own —— there are many ways to think about origin —— I frequently seek out the assistance of others —— I wonder if I will eventually become inured to my condition —— the way explorers acclimate to the thin air up high —— that fringe of the body's ability to breathe —— I woke up in a sweat convinced I was elsewhere —— a tourist attraction at the back of my mind —— I dreamed I had found the book I'd misplaced

[THIS CONVICTION] [A TALE OF OUR WICKEDNESS / IT IS NOT] [

—— that I'd read the rest of the piece on the fringe —— it was full of war and art and piss —— the relationship of markers to sight —— I had coffee with a geographer in Boulder, Colorado —— the air was so thin I was gulping for breath —— he'd just returned from another trip to China —— we talked about Antin, Lippard, and my condition —— he made me feel totally, irrevocably soft —— we'll probably never see each other again —— later I wrote something down in my notebook —— it had to do with my questions about being a tourist —— and something the geographer had smilingly said —— returning is different from covering the same ground —— I held my coffee on one side with my hand from the other —— nervousness gestures to feeling's fringe —— the boy returned to the Gypsies every year for a decade —— the camp in Athens is now a seaside café —— if you want to be the one who goes back, go back —— I've no theory about how to be

OUR WICKEDNESS] /\/\/\//\ [IT WAS] [A PAIL OF PISS] [HE SAID

The government [should] subsidize struggling museums, theaters, and artists.

I [am] troubled by the eroding distinction between entertainment and marketing.

Protesters cause [more] good than harm.

A person [cannot] be truly spiritual without regularly attending church or temple.

Something like [the theory of natural selection] explains why some people are homeless.

If countries are unwilling to cooperate with our military plans, we should treat them as [enemies].

I feel guilty when I shop at a large national chain.

Social justice should be the foundation of any economic system.

People shouldn't be allowed to have children they can't provide for.

I would defend my property with lethal force.

The world would be better if there were no huge corporations.

Professional athletes are paid too much money.

The separation of church and state has demoralized our society.

The 'Word of God' exists only as human beings interpret it.

We need stronger laws protecting the environment.

I would feel better if there were video cameras on most street corners.

It should be legal for consenting adults to challenge each other to a duel.

SMILING AT HER GENTLY] [HIS BABY BLUE] [EYES] [IT WAS] /\/\/\/

I took a break from my condition to start translating a novel —— a story about neo-Nazis in Paris, France —— it's set in the late '90s, when I was living in Paris —— the protagonist and I lived on the very same street —— sometimes a place moves to the center of a life —— the author of the book is politically on the left —— my father lived through the occupations of Athens —— three times his home was taken over by soldiers —— the novel makes an argument about slippage at the extremes —— how it's possible to move effortlessly between far left and far right —— it offers as an example one Jacques Doriot —— communist mayor in the '30s of Saint-Denis —— a suburb of Paris at its northern fringe —— my father didn't talk about that part of his childhood —— I never could be sure that my impression of it was real —— there was one story he liked to tell about that time —— the story of Apostolos Santas, AKA Lakis —— who scaled the Acropolis in April of '41 —— tore down the Nazi flag and put nothing in its place —— a symbolic act for which he was sentenced to death in absentia —— Jacques Doriot turned fascist in 1936 —— he wore the ss uniform into his grave —— Saint-Denis hosts a campus of the University of Paris —— in 1991 I took some classes there —— the students it attracted were the self-described fringe —— the graffiti on the walls has been painted over since then —— I signed up for a class with a man named Vuarnet —— the title of

[YOU REMEMBER THAT OLD FIELD WE WENT TO AND WE SAT] [IN

the class was Philosophy and Art —— the name of the professor was spelled like the sunglasses —— at the time you could smoke and drink beer in the classroom —— Vuarnet kept his inside a brown paper bag —— Apostolos Santas did not act alone —— he captured the flag with Manolis Glezos —— who later led the Coalition of the Radical Left —— Apostolos died in 2011 —— a recipient of medals from the Greek state —— Manolis was arrested by Athens riot police —— as recently as October of 2012 —— when I was at Saint-Denis I kept a low profile —— Desert Storm was in force and I was still an American —— I marched for peace and wages with the thousands in the streets —— but nothing brought them out like the loss of March the second —— Lucien Ginsburg, the French-Ukranian who'd changed his name to Serge —— sometimes a voice moves the center to a halt —— when Lucien was a boy he wore the yellow star —— when he tried to be a singer he was mocked for his nose —— in the years that followed he moved as if inevitably toward the center —— in '75 he made an album that satirized the Nazis —— there's something I haven't told you that has to do with my condition —— the night Serge Gainsbourg died I heard all of Paris weeping —— when I cry I cry for these imperfect things

A RUINED PARLOR] [AND THEY AND WE TRIED] [TO IMAGINE] [

If someone is crying, you [Avert your eyes]

If you think someone's ugly, you [Tank top and shorts]

If someone picks up a lost purse, you [Tell them that you trust everyone]

If your friend asks you who you trust the most, you [Only if the situation required it]

If you are going to church, you wear [10–15 times]

If you are very religious, and someone who follows a different religion preaches to you, you [   ]

In average, how often do you lie a day?

Would you tell a white lie to make someone feel better?

What saying would you say you most often follow?

Which of the following is the correct definition of 'moral'?

THAT WE BELONGED TO THESE TIMES—THEY ARE DEAD AND WE ARE

My condition is rare but it still affects thousands —— it's easy to feel like I'm being punished by god —— not believing in god can have damaging consequences —— the source of punishment tends to revert to the self —— self-punishment is the base of many social dynamics —— a sense of conscience can be wielded from within or without —— the Gypsies hold a Kantian belief about ethics —— this according to the European who spent his youth among them —— wherein stealing is judged permissible according to intent —— it is possible that I can make peace with my condition —— if I can convince myself its intent is benign —— there's a mediation technique called nonviolent communication —— conventionally known as NVC —— I try to use it in relation to my desire to be cured —— the goal is to do away with judgments of value —— and focus on everyone's needs being met —— the relation of the 'Gypsy code' to Kant is as follows —— for Kant a right action is spoiled by impure intent —— this aligns well with the NVC model —— in which an act of generosity is immediately voided —— if revealed to be spurred by resentment or guilt —— for the boy's Gypsies, stealing was morally neutral —— as long as nobody's needs were denied —— take one chicken from the farmer but not the whole coop —— there are many ways to think about dessert —— this neutrality was voided if greed entered the picture —— NVC holds a broad

] [NOT DEAD, WE ARE DEAD AND THEY ARE NOT] [DEAD] [AND

understanding of violence —— it would encompass even my own relation to my condition —— my conscience tells me empathy for the self is undeserved —— the website contains an inventory of needs —— which are neatly divided into seven subsections —— that begin with connection and end with meaning —— this positioning of meaning calls out my condition —— my needs are out of date

acceptance	trust	freedom
affection	warmth	independence
appreciation		space
belonging	air	spontaneity
cooperation	food	
communication	movement/exercise	awareness
closeness	rest/sleep	celebration of life
community	sexual expression	challenge
companionship	safety	clarity
compassion	shelter	competence
consideration	touch	consciousness
consistency	water	contribution
empathy		creativity
inclusion	authenticity	discovery
intimacy	integrity	efficacy
love	presence	effectiveness
mutuality		growth
nurturing	joy	hope
respect/self-respect	humor	learning
safety		mourning
security	beauty	participation
stability	communion	purpose
support	ease	self-expression
to know and be known	equality	stimulation
to see and be seen	harmony	to matter
to understand and be understood	inspiration	understanding
	choice	

The title of this poem doesn't come from 'the fringe' —— but from the name of the book in which it appears —— and a talk therein that shares that name —— that served as a balm when there was no cure —— the Roma are said to be bonded by language —— the Greeks were bonded by language too —— the ancients were and the moderns are —— Antin's right that the light makes it hard to see —— my condition has something to do with this too —— I was wrong about the profession of the Belgian boy's parents —— his father was an artist who worked in stained glass —— who trained as a painter under Gustave Moreau —— his mother's described as an 'artsy pacifist' —— my father has since told me all he remembers —— the boy was a man when he left the Gypsies —— he was arrested by the gestapo in 1943 —— he moved to New York to start a family —— by 1959 he was living in Hell's Kitchen —— I wonder if he and Antin met on the fringe —— my father's mother marched up and challenged the soldiers —— my mother's mother had my condition too —— I write to the cook when another friend dies —— I type what would an ethical happiness look like —— 'the fringe' ends with a pail of Guggenheim piss —— the list ends with twenty-one meanings of 'meaning' —— I finished the translation but the work doesn't end —— it will end —— it moves inevitably toward its end

IS NOT DEAD] [SOMETHING IS HAPPENING] [IN THE ROOM] [

THERE BE TROUBLE \\/\\\\/ VIBRATION /\\/ INSIDE THE] [MACHINE] [

FLAT WHITE
(20/20)

a compromised translation

with, and for, Samira Negrouche

A RADIUS OF ONE \/ UNCOUNTABLE / WE CANNOT IMAGINE /\ WE

IMAGINE] [ACCOUNTABLE] [FORCE] [ΝΟΥΣ OR NOUS] [ONE OR

{1}

There are the pages that arrive without your writing them
at the end of the night that an editor won't expect that
forge a path toward an imaginary book you watch recede
as time goes by you prefer to think of it forever inside the
dead memory of the computer.

{2}

I like to drink coffee with a cloud of fake cream I like
coffee without anything without sugar I only like when
the thick cloud of dawn I confront before sleep when it
slides and collapses the valleys from the hills and in
silence I like this trickle of cream it transports me / from
breast unto nípple / from breast to breast.

{3}

She served me a watery cup in a bowl the color of earth
she said I've written a novel but the diskette is broke she
said look at my olive trees I have dreamed of an orchard /\
long I walk /\ down three steps I see weeds in the distance
ablaze in the sun a lemon tree bent in defense like a blind
forward /\ on the football field /\ I say it's handsome your
field /\ of olives try a new brand of diskette.

{4}

One two count the drops that fall from the sky on the
insolent plastic that litters the balcony three four all
thoughts are worth the pursuit when nothing will come
not desire not sleep I look /\ sidelong for a cigarette \/\ I
don't even \ smoke.

{5}

Rue Didouche Mourad midnight thirty-five the two men
walk up say we'll walk til we get to the end til we become
young til it's the twenty-third century I say the poets are
mad it's a good thing these two exist we'll go they say /\
on camelback /\ til in the desert while waiting I'll be made
to tránslate /\ make flesh /\ the turns—say virages—that
have loaned me \\/\ have taken me on loan.

LIKE] [OPTIMISM] [TO BE IN THE WAY OF] [SOMETHING LIKE] [

{6}

Cats don't need anyone to whisper in their ears they don't
circle their bowls they wait patiently then furiously on the
disordered dresser they curl up with dexterous skill the
perfect distance from the radiator you haven't lifted your
foot they know already if you'll fidget or get up.

HAPPINESS] [AIRLESS] [THE ROOM] [BECOMES ONLY] [THE TRAG-

{7}

Again this hand that trembles that can barely put vulgar
pen to crossword grid the piano still /\ shut and dusty the
poet a scared shadow on a stripped easy chair that faces
the extinguished streetlamp of a sleeping mosque and
dreams of the day that will arrive without him.

{8}

I say that to write the most banal things you must first
write of your birth of your mother of your father of the
love of bodies of women of men of rapists and assassins
of incest and night sweats and of the hunger of the desert
of books of envy of suspicion of sex of ruins of the sea of
trees of archaeology of the Greek and Pagan gods and of
the stars I say all of this is almost banal before you write
and after.

LEAVES IT] [OPEN] [AND US] [TO RADICAL] [MOISTURE] [OR] [

{ 1 }

Samira it's dark outside and winter the branches are thick
with snow I think where there are deserts and olives there
can't be snow but California my mother /\ land gives me
the lie.

{ 2 }

Samira I have questions I'm afraid to ask like what does it
mean je traverse du sein au téton which I translated first
as from breast to tit like a girl coming out ontological
shift the discovery of eros and then later as something /\
else I'm afraid to ask after the ratio of banal to dramatic
in your day or your year /\ my fear \/ soft like a cat that
swings its tail //\ in irritation while asking to be pet.

{9}

You have to multiply the word mountain by quick and avid breaths retain that which might resemble an oxygenic dizziness like a veritable frontier between the states of mourning and of resurrection.

{ 3 }

I have read that language / leaves \ that it leaves a trace //
ok \ 'I draw a /\ line' Samira the security system of this
translation has been compromised.

{10}

To slide between the dead leaves of a late winter and let yourself roll /\ your knees out of joint and muscles rusted deaf to all movement the animal mineral climbs and falls with a certain sensation of existing to kiss the horizon.

{ 4 }

I have a problem Samira with the title of your book in
which I found this poem /\ Le Jazz d'oliviers /\ or Jazz of
the Olive Trees I delete the 'the' but that doesn't fix 'jazz'
which although I'm quite sure you're referring to music
to the way your phrasings are improvisatory the way they
necessitate quick and avid /\ breaths how if you were a
wind player you'd do circular breathing or speak through
your clarinet like Anthony Braxton but the problem with
'jazz' isn't Braxton or the clarinet the problem is Broadway
and fourth grade dance class have you never /\ heard of a
thing called jazz hands—

[OF CIGARETTES IN THE ROOM] [PASS THEM] [AROUND] [STARE

{ 5 }

Samira you are my third Samira.

{11}

I like this place de la comédie where actors come and go
from Line 1 of the tram I sip a glass of whatever liquid's
turned warm in my hands and await the fall of night I live
my own little drama amidst silhouettes of the free and
self-confident I blame /\/ culture shock and wish for a
certain how do you say

{ 6 }

insouciance. Samira there's no word for the word virage
a bend turn curve or shift as in the language turn or the
ethical turn or the turn we are in the midst of now or as I
read in another window in an attempt to triangulate sense
a road full of dangerous bends / to go into a bend / to take
a bend / blind bend / about-turn and /\ finally /\ positive
reaction.

{ 7 }

The first Samira was delivered somehow by the Shah
was a straight-A student had the voice of an angel she
taught me to eat burned-bottom rice we were twelve and
thirteen how do you say assimilable she was cast against
type in Bye Bye Birdie she belted 'How Lovely to Be a
Woman' we studied chemistry drank coffee while I chain-
smoked Camel Lights we read The Stranger we learned
hell is other people we listened to Killing an Arab I think
she was voted most friendly / now practices / law in the
Bay I don't know /\ I don't know if she still goes /\ by Sam.

NOT KNOW HOW // STUPID TO SAY MERELY / THAT POETS SHOULD

{ 8 }

Samira I await your response to my queries I am in the
meantime translating interviews with Bresson he says
things I /\ admire /\ he likes / to work with amateurs has
coherent unpopular ideas says the value of an image is an
exchange / value /\ an image a word in the grammar of a
/ scene / he says aim for the emotion you want to produce
then do whatever /\ whatever /\ you veritably can.

{ 9 }

I want to tell you Samira how it is right now a small
stack of books on my desk their covers all red by a happy
coincidence one is yours In the Shadow of Grenada or In
the Shade of Granada I haven't worked on it yet but the top
one was published in 1968 /\ Disease, Pain, & Sacrifice:
Toward a Psychology of Suffering \/ and when I open it
here in front of you across the world I see the word pain
multiplied on the page /\ Pain as a Demand upon a Higher
Telos and The Phenomenally Ego-Alien Nature of Pain
and at the top The Paradox of the Function of Pain and we
know that pain pronounced pan spells bread in \ one of
your / extramaternal \ tongues // I read it \/ whose I is this
anyway \\/\ read it first as In the Shadow of the Grenade.

OTHERS] [WHO WAIT IN THOUR] [UNIFORMS] [STUPID] [FOR

{12}

Sometimes I think I should cast off now take the first boat
the first plane the first whatever just leave with swinging
arms with solitary heart with the feeling that the world is
immense I cross the boulevard of the port I hear the boat
howl I try to distract myself I almost crush a passerby and
I say to myself that Algiers is a whore I /\ mean by that /\
that she is a \ sacrée putain.

{ 10 }

The second Samira was in Baltimore she made mosaics
of glass came from Tunisia via France was pregnant when I
moved into the spare room she said she hoped it would
be a son //\ I would like to believe a girl could win she said
\ what I remember is all that I know \ and went on //\ but
a girl's life is nothing but pain \// the child was born male
they named it Loul /\ Arabic \ for 'one' he crawled into my
bed laughed himself to sleep when I left she was pregnant
again with a girl they named \/ her Naila the name of the
wife of the caliph Uthman who tried to prevent rebels
from murdering her husband \/\/ whose fingers were cut
off in the process \ who failed to prevent the murder of
her husband /\ I look up the meaning of Naila /\\/ 'the one
who wins.'

[SHOWN] [TO CORRELATE POSITIVELY] [W/ LEFT FRONTAL CORTEX

{13}

I would like to believe that the future will be bitter now that we need photos that fit to the millimeter on a pale crimson background to cross the Mediterranean and a stationary / bicycle to soften the Achilles /\ heel while waiting for lawns to be aerated in a yearly rotation and forests //\\ cleared by the false /\ fires of July.

{14}

I would be happy in the fashion of Prévert to encounter
the mysteries of New York and then the mysteries of Paris
and why not make a lament of my small demons my large
/\ my large / my even larger / caprices.

{ 11 }

I say that to write the most banal things you must first
write of your [   ] of your [   ] of your [   ] of the
love of [   ] of [   ] of [   ] of [   ] and [   ]
of [   ] and [   ] [   ] and of the [   ] of the [   ]
of [   ] of [   ] of [   ] of [   ] of [   ] of the [   ] of
[   ] of [   ] of the [   ] and [   ] [   ] and of
the [   ] I say all of this is almost [

{15}

Tomorrow is a day of which no one wants to think /
anymore for tomorrow traverses \ the hours / takes up
position at the window without /\ patienting for the moon
to fall.

{16}

The painter tells me that books are signs for me they are
nothing but the scrawlings of creatures in the space of my
screen since I've divorced myself from Arabic calligraphy
I'm afraid that the mountain of books will transform itself
to a wave of indecipherable signs.

{ 12 }

In an email you list your languages only Kabyle until you
were four then Arabic in school then French because you
asked /\ you mention the posited relation between Kabyle
and Greek /\ I look it up I find Sanskrit between them /\ I
find /\ that among Kabyle speakers there is no consensus
about which alphabet to use \//\ even /\ about the orienta-
tion of the line /\/\ I find the alphabet called Neo-Tifinagh
to be beautiful you say yes /\ it's beautiful you say you find
it /\ so.

TO SAY] [THAT THE PROBLEM] [IS REAL] [TO ASK] [WHOSE I IS

{ 13 }

That which predisposes toward an encounter that which
is meant by the argument against a private /\ language
that which is presented as an argument against empathy
that which joins the passions into a com /\ passion when
I translate your words using nonhuman means into an
alphabet whose calligraphy I don't know I have reason /\
to question /\ the accuracy of the result especially words
like sex and ruins like Pagan like incest like rapist and
suspicion I am willing to be wrong I stand / corrected
most of the time Samira I would prefer not to be wrong /
about certain /\ terms /\ among them 'night sweats' with
which I am \ familiar thanks to my / thanks to everyone's
/\ condition.

{ 14 }

first must you things banal most the write to that say I
the of //\/\/\ your of ////\\/\ your of \/\/\/\/ your of write
\/\/\/\/ and /\/\/\/\// of \/\/\/\\\ of /\/\/\/ of \/\/ of love
//\/\//\/ the of \/\//\//\\ the of and \/\/\/\/\/ \/\// and /\/\\/ of
of \//\ the of //\/\/\\ of \/\/\///\/\ of //\/\\/\//\/\ of \/\// of /\/\/ of
of and \/\/\/\/ //\/\/\ and \/\/\/\\\ the of /\/\\////\/\/ of \/\/
before banal almost //\//\/\/\/\/\/\//\ is this of all say I \/\/ the

{ 15 }

I say the future will be bitter I did not say better say better
/ Samira do you ever start writing \ one \ and end up /\
static / with another \/ other.

{17}

She makes the gesture for writing she says tell me what
happened one day she says tell me this in the present and
execute sound bites I say my memory is overloaded there
is too much going on or not enough in a day how to peel
the onion of Günter Grass how to press the alarm bell /
to go in / the day that counts on words that / count / how
to stare at the truth of this moment /\ that is /\ the birth
of the abortion / \\/\/\//\/ the abortion of language.

{18}

I too would like to know what happened one day in the present to relive all this but on this day / today \ I am really really tired.

{19}

There is when sleep abandons you something on the order
of an injustice / of \ a madness.

{ 16 }

I woke up with night sweats and a realization /\ the second Samira wasn't Samira at all \ but Samia / it's been seventeen years no excuse \/ she is back in Tunisia with her family now does this \\/ mean we can change things that things can change /\ Samira \ in Greek my father tongue the word for today is simera /\ I loved her forgot her \ name \/\ I guess \/ I too am tired \ really really tired.

{ 17 }

The Roma say feri ando payi stsholpe te nay nas /\ or /\
in the water one learns to swim /\ and the Greeks say δεν
ντρέπεσαι \ aren't you ashamed \ but in Greece this is
meant affectionately \\ a joke /\ this is religious /\ I call
this religious difference.

{ 18 }

The title of your poem is Café Sans Sucre I tried Black
Coffee I tried Coffee, Black I tried Milk No Sugar when I
got to the reference to cream I remembered Australians
make a flat white I tried Flat White /\ at a reading and
somebody laughed /\ then I learned of the flat white
economy in London \/\ flat meaning affect and white
meaning White used metonymically if not intentionally
for settlers /\/\ and as is often the case I don't know which
sense to keep.

{ 19 }

The number of olive trees uprooted by settlers has reached /\ 800,000 \\/ the professor who coined the term 'flat white economy' has been charged / for attacking a prostitute / white //\ after smoking crack /\ which she tried to turn down \/ Samira I want your poem to flatten my \/ all of my veritable signs.

{ 20 }

They grow olives in California too / I order oil by the gallon when I don't forget \ it's labeled organic it's limited / edition \/\ Samira / we are not perfect /\ friends by definition / not above /\ reproach / I stand / corrected /\ attempt to triangulate /\ the individual's coordinates /\/\/\ amidst the group.

TRIANGULAR] [IT FLIES IN ITS] [DREAMS] [ITS COLOR IS THE

{20}

That which predisposes toward an encounter these
are sometimes the four winds that become confused /
telescope / on an eagle's nest and the instant /\ word of love
will cancel \/ really cancels /\ all the forces of opposition.

COLOR OF] [AIR] \/\/ \\ / [ITS TITLE IS 'KITE'] [IT IS A] [KITE]

//\/\/\/\\/\/\   \\/ \ // \\ / \ ///   \\\ /\/\/\/   //\//\/\/\/\\/\/   /\//\

///////   ///////////   //////   ///   ///   ////////////////

NOTES

'Flat White (20/20)' began as an act of 'straight' translation and then morphed into something else. I am grateful to the Algerian poet, editor, and translator Samira Negrouche for being open to, and colluding with, my interventions in her text. The resulting piece comprises my often-corrupt translations of the twenty sections of Samira's poem (indicated by numbers between unspaced brackets) interspersed with twenty sections I wrote in response (indicated by numbers between spaced brackets). The book in which Samira's original poem appears is *Le jazz des oliviers* (Editions du Tell, Blida, 2010).

In 'What It Means to Be Avant-Garde,' my usage of 'Gypsies' and 'Roma' refers to the usage of these terms in Jan Yoors's book, my memory of which engendered and troubles the poem. In the same poem, the 'needs inventory' on page 46 was taken from the website of the Center for Nonviolent Communication, © 2005.

These poems were written under the influence of (and sometimes quote) texts by David Antin, Teresa Brennan, Robert Bresson, Aimé Césaire, Theresa Hak Kyung Cha, Didier Daeninckx, Hubert Dreyfus, Ellie Ga, Søren Kierkegaard, Lucy Lippard, Dean MacCannell, David Markson, George Oppen, Adam Phillips, Marshall Rosenberg, Eve Kosofsky Sedgwick, Ngũgĩ wa Thiong'o, Aglaja Veteranyi, and Jan Yoors; the Romani folio from Drunken Boat, edited by T. M. De Vos; and various self-tests found online.

\|/// \|//\ /\|\|/ //\|//\ / \|/\|//\|\|/\|/\|/ \|/ \| /\| //\|/

///\/\//   ///\ /\ // \\/ \ / /\   /\   \/\/ \\   /\\/   /

ACKNOWLEDGMENTS

Portions and/or versions of these poems first appeared in *Dusie, The Volta Book of Poets, Vanitas,* and *A Public Space.* Thanks to the editors, and to the George A. and Eliza Gardner Howard Foundation, Writers OMI, the Abbeye de Lérins, the Fund for Poetry, and Tamaas for their support. For editorial reads or otherwise essential engagement with these poems, thanks to Anselm Berrigan, Pam Dick, Natalie Eilbert, Hope Hall, Ann Lauterbach, Ben Lerner, Rachel Levitsky, Samira Negrouche, Michael Nicoloff, Simone White, Matvei Yankelevich, and the Spring 2015 'multilingualisms' class in the Pratt MFA in writing. Thanks also to everyone at Coffee House Press and to Sean, Samia, Sam, and all my friends and family, especially Trevor Wilson.

In memory of Gertrude Jewell Stevenson Rand (1898–1969), Ismene Bistis Moschovakis (1908–2008), Lenny, Easley, Rituraj, and Sasha.

/\|/\|\| /\|/\ \|\|\|/ /\|/\|/ /\|\|\| /\ /\ \|\|/   /   \|//\   \|/

/|| / | |/| //|

Coffee House Press began as a small letterpress operation in 1972 and has grown into an internationally renowned nonprofit publisher of literary fiction, essay, poetry, and other work that doesn't fit neatly into genre categories.

Coffee House is both a publisher and an arts organization. Through our *Books in Action* program and publications, we've become interdisciplinary collaborators and incubators for new work and audience experiences. Our vision for the future is one where a publisher is a catalyst and connector.

LITERATURE
is not the same thing as
PUBLISHING

FUNDER ACKNOWLEDGMENTS

Coffee House Press is an internationally renowned independent book publisher and arts nonprofit based in Minneapolis, MN; through its literary publications and *Books in Action* program, Coffee House acts as a catalyst and connector—between authors and readers, ideas and resources, creativity and community, inspiration and action.

Coffee House Press books are made possible through the generous support of grants and donations from corporate giving programs, state and federal support, family foundations, and the many individuals who believe in the transformational power of literature. This activity is made possible by the voters of Minnesota through a Minnesota State Arts Board Operating Support grant, thanks to the legislative appropriation from the arts and cultural heritage fund and a grant from the Wells Fargo Foundation Minnesota. Coffee House also receives major operating support from the Amazon Literary Partnership, the Bush Foundation, the Jerome Foundation, the McKnight Foundation, Target, and the National Endowment for the Arts (NEA). To find out more about how NEA grants impact individuals and communities, visit www.arts.gov.

Coffee House Press receives additional support from many anonymous donors; the Alexander Family Foundation; the Archer Bondarenko Munificence Fund; the Elmer L. & Eleanor J. Andersen Foundation; the David & Mary Anderson Family Foundation; the Buuck Family Foundation; the Carolyn Foundation; the Dorsey & Whitney Foundation; Dorsey & Whitney LLP; the Knight Foundation; the Rehael Fund of the Minneapolis Foundation; the Schwab Charitable Fund; Schwegman, Lundberg & Woessner, P.A.; the Scott Family Foundation; the US Bank Foundation; VSA Minnesota for the Metropolitan Regional Arts Council; the Archie D. & Bertha H. Walker Foundation; and the Woessner Freeman Family Foundation.

THE PUBLISHER'S CIRCLE OF COFFEE HOUSE PRESS

Publisher's Circle members make significant contributions to Coffee House Press's annual giving campaign. Understanding that a strong financial base is necessary for the press to meet the challenges and opportunities that arise each year, this group plays a crucial part in the success of Coffee House's mission.

Recent Publisher's Circle members include many anonymous donors, Mr. & Mrs. Rand L. Alexander, Suzanne Allen, Patricia A. Beithon, Bill Berkson & Connie Lewallen, the E. Thomas Binger & Rebecca Rand Fund of the Minneapolis Foundation, Robert & Gail Buuck, Claire Casey, Louise Copeland, Jane Dalrymple-Hollo, Mary Ebert & Paul Stembler, Kaywin Feldman & Jim Lutz, Chris Fischbach & Katie Dublinski, Katharine Freeman, Sally French, Jocelyn Hale & Glenn Miller, Roger Hale & Nor Hall, Randy Hartten & Ron Lotz, Jeffrey Hom, Carl & Heidi Horsch, Kenneth Kahn & Susan Dicker, Stephen & Isabel Keating, Kenneth Koch Literary Estate, Jennifer Komar & Enrique Olivarez, Allan & Cinda Kornblum, Leslie Larson Maheras, Jim & Susan Lenfestey, Sarah Lutman & Rob Rudolph, Carol & Aaron Mack Charitable Fund of the Minneapolis Foundation, George & Olga Mack, Joshua Mack, Gillian McCain, Mary & Malcolm McDermid, Sjur Midness & Briar Andresen, Peter Nelson & Jennifer Swenson, Marc Porter & James Hennessy, Jeffrey Scherer, Jeffrey Sugerman & Sarah Schultz, Maureen Millea Smith & Daniel Smith, Marla Stack & Dave Powell, Nan G. & Stephen C. Swid, Patricia Tilton, Stu Wilson & Melissa Barker, Warren D. Woessner & Iris C. Freeman, Margaret Wurtele, and Joanne Von Blon.

For more information about the Publisher's Circle and other ways to support Coffee House Press books, authors, and activities, please visit www.coffeehousepress.org/support or contact us at info@coffeehousepress.org.

ABOUT THE AUTHOR

Anna Moschovakis lives and works in the Catskill Mountains and in New York City.

They and We Will Get into Trouble for This

is set in Warnock Pro and Optima,

with titles set in Scala Sans.